Heraldry
from its Historic Origins
by
Hugh Murray

INTRODUCTION

As a general rule books on heraldry take the present state of the art as their starting point and give scant attention to its gradual evolution over the 800 or more years of its existence. While the language of blazon, the rules of marshalling and the accoutrements that form an heraldic achievement are dealt with in detail there is usually little attempt to describe the development of heraldry from a simple shield decoration to a full achievement with mantling, torse, supporters, motto, headgear, helm, crest, and decorations. Some books are, of course, better than others. *The Oxford Guide to Heraldry* is outstanding in this respect but does not answer all the questions. A knowledge of when and how these additions were introduced and eventually formally adopted is an essential part of the subject.

The identification of an armigerous family from the charges and tinctures on a particular representation of a coat of arms often fails to reveal which member of the family is intended. A knowledge, then, of when the shield shape in the drawing was introduced or when the colours of mantling changed from *gules* and *argent* to the principle colour and metal of the blazon may allow the achievement to be dated more precisely. This knowledge in turn will allow the elimination of some members of the family and may, in the best case, identify the actual person.

An artist, asked to produce the achievement for a particular person, can, with a knowledge of the history of heraldry, avoid introducing anachronisms into the design. The finished result will be thus the more authentic.

It is to solve problems of this sort that, over the years since my interest in heraldry was stimulated, I have accumulated references to the introduction of various heraldic and ancillary practices and their adoption and modification in use. I am sure others have been equally frustrated in their attempts to find this historical information and it is to them I offer the results of my jottings, now formalised and indexed. I make no claim to originality or new research. Nearly all my knowledge has come from the works of others and so that users of this treatise can move one stage nearer the authority for a particular statement and check it for themselves I have given full references of my sources. These take the form of two numbers separated by a comma, for example [21,344]. The first number identifies the book (see Appendix) in which the particular fact has been found and the second the page number in that book.

INDEX

HERALDRY

12th C First known appearance of formal heraldry. In 1127 Henry I presented his son–in–law, Geoffrey of Anjou, on the occasion of his marriage, a shield figured with little gold lions. After Geoffrey's death in 1150 an enamel plate was placed in the cathedral at Le Mans. On this plate is his effigy holding a shield which appears to be blazoned *azure 6 lions rampant or*. These arms were subsequently used by his grandson, William Longespee (died 1226), and his great grand–daughter, Adela, Countess of Warwick. [36,16]

The impetus for the development of heraldry was the Crusades, started in 1095 and the simultaneous development of tournaments. In both cases it was necessary for the participants to be recognizable to each other and their supporters.[5,4/5]

THE SHIELD

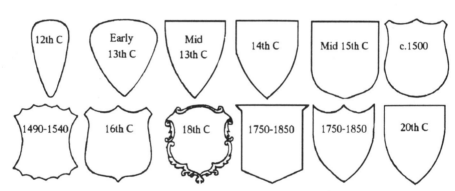

Shape [24,76/77]

12th–14th C	The heraldic shield followed the shape actually used in warfare
1270	Lozenges used for the display of arms on seals.[12,62]
1296	Roundels used for the display of arms on seals.[12,62]
15th C	As heraldic design became more complicated heraldic shields became more rectangular to allow the charges to be properly displayed.
1490–1540	Rectangular and waisted shield with foliage at top and bottom in use.[23,24]
17th & 18th C	Elaborate rococo shield shapes are commonly used bearing no relationship to those ever in actual use.
19th C	The movement back to a recognizable conventional shield for the display of charges begins.
20th C	The College of Arms returns to the medieval heater shaped shield for normal displays of heraldic charges.

1

Shape for Women

1561/2 A Chapter of the Officers of Arms settled on the use of a lozenge for the display of arms by single or widowed women.[12,55] Prior to this the lozenge had merely been a variation of shield shape in general use, for example, on the seals of Thomas Furnival, died 1279,[19,38] or William Paynell, 1301,[20,112] (see right).

Blazon

By c1255 Principal terms and conventional order of blazon crystallized. Blazon in Norman French but occasionally Latin.[31,17]

c1430 Occasional use of gems for tinctures – a system invented by Sicily Herald.[35,77] Planets and virtues as tincture names also introduced at this time.[38,53]

By 2nd half of 15th C English blazon introduced with Norman French terms anglicized.[31,17]

16th C The fashion of avoidance of repetition in blazon came in – using terms like 'of the field' or 'of the second' to avoid repeating tinctures.[31,112]

Tinctures

15th C Introduction of terms colour and metal[31,105 &110]

16th C Introduction of the term fur for the varieties of ermine and vair.[31,107]

1562 Language of Colour described.[22,fo.1]

17th C Introduction of the term 'tincture' to cover, inclusively, the colours metals and furs.[31,113]

Tricking

Early 16th C Tricked shields, indicating tinctures by letters, used in the notebooks compiled by the Kings of Arms on the visitations to their heraldic provinces.[31,113]

Hatching

1600 System of hatching to indicate tinctures first appeared in Langruis' Map of Brabant.[31,113]

1638 System of hatching popularized by Father de Petra Sancta in his *Tesserae Gentilitia*.[31,113]

1649 First use of hatching in England – on the death warrant of Charles I. [27,40]

HELMS

Early 13th Invention of closed helm

c1600 Rules for helms, when used as part of an achievement to indicate the rank of the bearer (monarch, peer, knight, gentleman), evolved during reign of Elizabeth I.[31,108]

| c1980 | Rule for helms relaxed by College of Arms to allow helms to be turned sideways or forward to allow the logical display of a sideways or forward facing crest.[4,vi] |

CRESTS

1150	Precursor of the crest to be seen on the headgear of Geoffrey of Anjou on his brass at Le Mans.
1198	First appearance of a recognizable crest on the 2nd Great Seal of Richard I.[7,254]
End of 14th C	Crests in general use.[37,27]
1561/2	It was decreed that women should not bear crests.[12,55]
5 June 1817	Warrant of Deputy Earl Marshal forbidding transmission of a crest by a woman.[38,76]

If a person has two crests the senior is placed to the dexter, if three the principal is placed in the centre, the second to the dexter and the third to the sinister.[38,85]

TORSE

| Mid 14th C | First appearance – a twisted scarf, possibly a lady's favour – of two colours not related to shield colours. |
| End of 16th | The blazon included the words 'on a wreath of the colours', the principal tinctures of the shield (those first used in the blazon). If one of them is a fur the dominant colour of the fur is used.[14,379] |

MANTLING

A small mantle or cloak hanging from the helm and draped down the back – perhaps to deflect the heat of the sun.

Mid 14th C	First appearance – no rule as to the colours at this time.
16th to 18th C	The tinctures gules and argent used for all except peers and royalty who early used gules and ermine.
Since early 18th C	Mantling picks up the principal tinctures of the shield (those mentioned first in the blazon).[31,110]
1741	The arms of peers in Collin's *Peerage of England* no longer shown with ermine lined mantling. This has remained the practice until the present day.[38,89]
1953	Ruling by Kings of Arms – Badges may be shown on mantling but no unauthorized charges.[38,90]

| 1957 | Ruling by Kings of Arms – Furs and Proper are neither metal nor colour.[38,90] |

SUPPORTERS

Beginning	Practice of filling the spaces on either side of shields on seals begins [31,16]. of 14th C
2nd half of 14th C	These infillers evolved into recognizable supporters. [20,260]
2nd quarter of 15th C[5,211]	First definite use of supporters in the time of Henry VI.[5,211]
Beginning of 16th C	Supporters confined to peers and knights of principal orders.[31,16] Gentry allowed to retain them if of ancient use.[38,101]

Seal of John, Earl of Arundel, 1432

MOTTOES

Mottoes probably derive from war cries but later became pious hopes or sentiments.

| 1293 | The motto *Crede Beronti* used by Sir John de Byron on his seal. [38,112] |
| 18th C | In general use – earlier examples are generally for peers.[9,449] |

CROWNS and CORONETS

Coronets worn by Monarchs

before 1399	A circlet of trefoils or fleur de lys.
1399	The circlet was arched over.
1485	An arched over circlet of alternate crosses and fleur de lys.[20,290]

Mural and Naval Crowns

Used in personal arms granted to distinguished soldiers and sailors respectively (generals, admirals and higher ranks only). Both appear in civic heraldry – the latter particularly for seaports.[7,279]

1617	Mural crown displayed with arms of City of York on a chair in Wakefield Cathedral.
1652	Crest with a mural crown granted to the City of Gloucester.[9,322]
1658	Grant of arms including a naval crown to the family of Lendon.[25,185]
1797	Augmentation including naval crown granted to Admiral Adam Duncan for his victory at Camperdown.[21,88/9]
1815	Crest of augmentation including a mural crown granted to Field Marshal Sir John Byng for services in the Peninsular War and at Waterloo.[21,107–9]
1914	Mural crown granted to the London County Council instead of a crest, a precedent followed for later county councils.[5,188]

Coronets worn by Peers

1362	Coronets for Dukes introduced at the investiture of Lionel, son of Edward III, as Duke of Clarence.[20,272]
1385	Robert de Vere, Earl of Oxford, created Marquess of Dublin and invested with a circlet of gold.[20,272]
Temp Eliz I	Privilege of wearing a coronet extended to Viscounts. Distinctive pattern of coronets for peers above the rank of Baron evolved.[31,105]
7 Aug 1661	Royal warrant allowed Barons to wear a distinctive coronet.[31,105]

PEERS

Duke

1337   Norman title of Duke revived when Edward, the Black Prince, created Duke of Cornwall by his father, Edward III.[16,224]

Premier Duke of			
	England	Norfolk	created 1483
	Scotland	Hamilton	created 1643
	Ireland	Leinster	created 1766

Marquess

1385   First Marquess (margrave) – Robert de Vere, Earl of Oxford, created Marquess of Dublin by Richard II.[16,414]

Premier Marquess of			
	England	Winchester	created 1551
	Scotland	Huntly	created 1599
	Ireland	Leinster	created 1766

Earl

A Saxon title, by tenure.[16,226]

Premier Earl Union Roll			
of Scotland	Crawford & Balcarres		created 1398
	Mar		created 1404
of England & Ireland			
	Shrewsbury & Waterford		created 1442
of England	Norfolk		created 1483
of Ireland	Leinster		created 1766

Viscount

1440   First Viscount, John, Lord Beaumont, created Viscount Beaumont by Henry VI.[16,680]

Premier Viscount			
	of Ireland	Gormanstown	created 1478
	of England	Hereford	created 1550
	of Scotland	Falkland	created 1620

Baron

A Norman title by tenure, although existing earlier as Vavasour and Thane (Saxon)

1205   Barons first summoned to Parliament

1265	Barons created by writ – first on record.
1387	Barons created by patent – the first, John of Beauchamp, Baron of Kidderminster, created by Richard II.[16,68]

Premier Baron   of Ireland   Kingscale   created 1223
           of England   Mowbray, Segrave & Stourton
                                      created 1283,1283 & 1448
           of Scotland   Forbes   created 1445

BARONETS

Left –Badge of a Baronet of the United Kingdom
Right – Badge of a Baronet of Nova Scotia

22 May 1611	Baronets of England created by James I in connection with the colonization of Ulster from those whose grandfathers in the male line were armigerous and had an income of at least £1000 a year. They could ensign their arms with an escutcheon bearing *a sinister hand appaumy gules.*
30 July 1619	Baronets of Ireland created. Baronets now referred to as 'of England and Ireland'.
26 May 1625	Baronets of Nova Scotia created by James I, before his death, and confirmed by Charles I in connection with the colonization of Nova Scotia. They could ensign their arms with an escutcheon bearing a St Andrew's Cross and the arms of Scotland. In all 109 were created.
1 May 1707	Union of English and Scottish Parliaments – no more baronets of Nova Scotia created after this date.
3 Dec 1783	No person to be created a baronet until his right to bear arms had been certified from College of Arms records.
1 Jan 1801	Union of English and Irish Parliaments. All subsequent creations entitled Baronets of the United Kingdom.[6 Vol 1,vii][16,68][26]

Premier Baronet	of England	Bacon	created 1611
	of Ireland	Sarsfield	created 1619
	of Nova Scotia	Gordon	created 1625

AUGMENTATIONS of HONOUR

An additional hereditary quarter, charge or crest granted to commemorate a particular event or service. They start to appear in the early 14th century.

Crest of Augmentation granted to Sir Francis Drake in 1581

1334	Sir Walter Manny was recorded at the Second Dunstable Tournament as bearing a royal lion (on the upper chevron) on his shield in addition to his normal three chevrons.[21,8]
1356	Sir John Pelham granted an additional quarter of two buckles for his part in capturing John, King of France

1385/6	(1350–64), at Poitiers.[21,16] This is spurious.[38,69]

1385/6 Additional quarter granted to Robert de Vere, 9th Earl of Oxford, as long as he held the lordship of Ireland.[38,69]

1646 Charles I gave Garter King of Arms power to grant augmentations. [21,7]

1660 Charles II, at the restoration of the monarchy, gave Garter King of Arms a warrant authorising him to grant augmentations (any of our royal badges) to add to arms. This is the authority for the present system of augmentations although in the 18th and 19th centuries many that were not royal badges were granted.[21,7]

A crest of augmentation takes the senior position to the dexter if two crests are used.[38,85]

MITRES

Worn by Archbishops, Bishops and certain Abbots. Not found before the 10th century and then only for Popes and Cardinals. In 11th century extended to Archbishops and Bishops, 1049–54, and Abbots, 1063. In 12th century used on seals.[17,60]

1345 An early possible heraldic use on the Palatinate seal of Thomas Hatfield, Bishop of Durham, 1345–81.

1438 A definite heraldic use on privy seal of Robert Nevill, bishop of Durham, 1438–57.[20,163]

HATS

Roman Catholic

1243–54 Pope Innocent IV granted hats to cardinals to distinguish them from other prelates.[17,68]

1313 A Cardinal's hat carved on the tomb of Cardinal Riccardo Petroni at Sienna above his arms.[17,69]

1405 Similar use on tomb of Cardinal Beaufort, Bishop of Winchester, in Southwark cathedral.[20,164]

17th C Pierre Palliot made one of the first attempts to systemize a hierarchy of hats.[17,70]

Left to right – Hats for a Cardinal, a Bishop and a Priest

1832 Sacred Congregation of Ceremonies fixed number of tassels on Cardinal's hats to 15 on each side.[17,69]

| 21 Feb 1905 | Most clerical hats brought under uniform control. There are still some irregularities among green hats.[17,70 & 157] |
| 17 July 1967 | Official use of Roman Catholic hats allowed in English heraldry for the personal arms of Roman Catholic clergy.[4,89] |

Anglican

| 21 Dec 1976 | Earl Marshal's warrant detailed a hierarchy of clerical hats for use by Anglican clergy to be used, if they wished, instead of a crest.[17,135] |

BADGES

An independent device which existed before armorial shields – a mark of allegiance or ownership which can be used where it is not lawful to use a coat of arms.

c1140	The planta genista – the badge of Geoffrey of Anjou.[5,163]
Temp Edward	Badges in general use.[8,12]
14th–16th C	Most prevalent period for the use of badges.[8,20]
18 June 1906	Practice of granting badges revived by Earl Marshal's warrant.[5,170]

CADENCY

It is a principle of English heraldry that a coat of arms should be distinctive not only of a family as a whole but also of its branches and individual members. Several systems were tried before the present one was arrived at.

Modification by the addition of a label

| Before 1219 | Earliest known label on the counter seal of Saer de Quincey, 1st Earl of Winchester (died 1219), younger brother of Robert de Quincey.[5,114] |

Modification of tinctures

| Temp Henry II | Two branches of the Furnival family were distinguished by *or* and *argent* fields. |
| 1216–72 | [5,109] |

Modification by the addition of ordinaries

| 1256–72 | Richard, Earl of Poictou and Cornwall and King of the Romans differenced his arms by the addition of a bordure for his earldom of Poictou.[27,187] Bends were also used for differencing. |

Modification by the addition of charges

| by 1317 | Sons of Peter de Mauley in the Mauley window, York Minster, are distinguished by the addition of charges (dolphins, wyvern, eagles and crosses crosslet) onto the bend. |

Differencing by the addition of single small marks

c1400   Sons of Thomas de Beauchamp, Earl of Warwick, in the windows of St Mary's church, Warwick, are distinguished by small marks added to the shield (label, crescent, annulet, rose, martlet and molet).[27,181/2]

c1500   Present system invented by Sir John Writhe, Garter King of Arms (1478–1504).[15,42] If a cadency mark appears on a shield it should also appear on the crest.[38,85]

Bastardy

17th C   Plain bordure used to denote non–royal illegitimacy.

19th C   Changed to wavy bordure.

A baton sinister is used in grants to natural children of a sovereign.[38,68]

Divorced Women

c1980   Recent practice allows a divorced woman to revert to her paternal arms differenced by a mascle.[38,116]

ARMORIAL MEMORIAL BOARDS

16th C   First appearance, possibly as a cheap form of memorial.[29,19]

HATCHMENTS

1629   Earliest known hatchment in England, at Eye, Herefordshire for John Blount – slightly earlier appearance in the Low Countries.[29,17 & 19]

1631   Hatchment in Marnhull church, Dorset, to Lieutenant Fillol.

1635   Hatchment in Long Melford church, Suffolk to Viscount Savage.

May 1987   Hatchment in Rowley church near Beverley for Canon Christopher Hildyard, patron of the living.

Dec 1987   Hatchment in Brandesburton church, near Beverley for Timothy Blackmore, killed in Columbia.

Nov 1990   Hatchment in St Mary, Hemel Hemstead, to Humphrey Lindsay (designed and painted by Michael Holmes).

Hatchment, Dec. 1987, at Brandesburton

9

MARSHALLING

Dimidiation to indicate marriage
c1195   Dimidiated arms on seal of Robert Pinkney.[30,112]

Impalement to indicate marriage or office
mid 14th C   Impalement replaces dimidiation as the means of conjoining the arms of a husband and wife.[12,41/2] Shortly afterwards the practice of impaling personal arms with the arms of an office began amongst senior clergy. In 1397 Archbishop Robert Waldby impaled his arms with those of the See of York on his seal for the regality of Hexham.

1590   Regius Professors at Cambridge allowed to impale their personal arms with those of their chairs.[19,37]

1660   Regular use of impaled arms by Kings of Arms.[38,119]

c1975   Heads of any arms bearing authority or organisation allowed to impale their personal arms with those of their organisation.[4,vii]

Others entitled to impale are Abbots, Deans of Cathedrals, Heads of Colleges, Lord Mayors, Mayors and Council Chairmen.

Escutcheon of Pretence for heiresses
17th C   Not in general use until this time[12,42], although earlier examples can be found as on the Garter stall plate of Sir Richard Beauchamp KG (1403) who, in 1423, married as his second wife, Isabel, sister and heir of Richard le Despencer.[18,Plate 34]

Canton for the heiress of her mother
1664   At Sir William Dugdale's visitation of Staffordshire he allowed Charles Cotton to record arms which included a Beresford quarter with Stanhope on a canton. His mother was heiress of her Beresford mother but not of her Stanhope father.[38,134]

Quartering
1291   Earliest known example of a quartered shield in England is on the tomb of Eleanor of Castile (died 1291), Queen of Edward I, at Westminster, although known elsewhere in 1230.[5,137][30,112]

Left – Arms of Eleanor of Castile
Right – Arms of Edward III

Temp Edw II   Earliest known instance of an English subject quartering arms is Sir Symon de
1308–11   Montagu.[5,137] His additional quarter represents arms acquired by marriage to an heiress.

| 1340 | Edward III quartered France (ancient) with England to reinforce his claim to the French throne.[5,207] Both this example and that of Eleanor of Castile represent a territorial acquisition or claim. |
| 1409 | Sir John Oldcastle quartered the arms of his wife, Joan Cobham. [38,123] |

ARCHITECTURAL DECORATION, STATUARY and STAINED GLASS

1219	Reclining effigy of William Marshall, Earl of Pembroke, in the Temple Church holding a shield.[42,20]
1247	Henry III ordered armorial glass for Rochester Castle – no longer extant [41,57]
c1250	Royal arms installed in a window in Chetwode church, Bucks.
c1253	Heraldic tiles in the Chapter House at Westminster Abbey – earliest surviving use of Royal arms as architectural decoration.[38,173]
1258	Henry III ordered arms to be carved in stone in the spandrels of the aisle arcades in Westminster Abbey – said to be the first use of heraldry in a permanent form as an architectural decoration.[38,173]
c1266	Heraldic stained glass installed in a chapel at Havering-atte–Bower.[38.173]
c1270	Heraldic stained glass installed in chapter house (now in west window) of Salisbury cathedral. The charges are individual pieces of glass leaded into the field.
1277	Shield of Arms on Brass of Sir John D'Abernon at Stoke D'Abernon.[42,41]
1285	Shields of Arms in arcading of the wooden chest tomb of John de Pitchford at Pitchford, Salop.[42,26]
1289	Heraldic Brass of Sir Roger de Trumpington at Chartham, Kent.[42,42]
1290	Shields of Arms in arcading of the chest tomb of Eleanor of Castile in Westminster Abbey.[42,26]
c1310	Earliest use of yellow stain gives glass painters the ability to use another colour other than black on a piece of glass.
Early 15th C	Use of abrasion of flashed ruby glass allows glass painters to expose the plain white glass beneath. This could then be stained yellow.
Late 15th C	First appearance of flashed azure glass.
c1540	First appearance in England of enamel paints of various colours allowing glass painters the freedom to paint complicated multi–quartered shields on one piece of glass.
Mid 17th C	General introduction of ledger slabs with incised inscription and heraldic achievement in deep relief [41,120] although earlier examples are known e.g. Henry Gray, died 1591, at Morpeth.

PURSUIVANTS, HERALDS and KINGS of ARMS

First mentions of the Officers of the College of Arms.[15]

1170	First record of heralds – as officials at jousts
1225	A person called Bond described as King of Heralds
c1276	Peter – Herald for North of Trent
c1334	Andrew – Clarenceaux King of Arms
1338	Windsor Herald
	Norroy King of Arms
1347	Lancaster Herald, herald to Earls and Dukes of Lancaster
c1393	John – Chester Herald, herald to Prince of Wales
30 June 1415	Office of Garter King of Arms created – William Bruges appointed
1418	Rouge Croix Pursuivant
1421	Richmond Herald, herald to John, Duke of Bedford
1448	Somerset Herald, herald to Edmund Beaufort, Duke of Somerset
	Blue Mantle Pursuivant
1484	York Herald
2 March 1484	First Formal Charter of College of Arms
1485	Rouge Dragon Pursuivant
c1490	Portcullis Pursuivant

GRANTS of ARMS

1418	Writ issued by Henry V stating that no-one should assume a coat of arms unless by proper grant or by inheritance from ancestors. Those who fought at Agincourt were exempt from this provision.[39,45/46]
1439	Earliest known grant of arms extant – to Drapers Company.[33,30]
1467	Right of Crown to issue patents of arms explicitly stated.[36,30]
1673	Grants in Northern Province to be made jointly by Garter & Norroy.
1680	Grants in Southern Province to be made jointly by Garter & Clarenceaux.[1,35]

ROLLS of ARMS

1244–59	Matthew Paris shields – earliest known collection of shields – as book illustration.[30,3 et seq.]
c1255	Glover's Roll – earliest known specific collection of English arms.[30,89 et seq.]
c1340	Cooke's Ordinary – earliest known ordinary (arms arranged by charge) in existence.[34,58]

VISITATIONS

Mid 15th C	Proto visitation of many shires and London by Roger Leigh, Clarenceaux King of Arms.[35,66]
19 Apr 1530	Royal proclamation of Henry VIII requiring Kings of Arms to visit their provinces to examine arms, reform them if necessary and destroy arms devised

without authority. Earliest Visitation under this order made by Thomas Benoit, Clarenceaux King of Arms in the same year. [35,55]

1687   Last visitation – made by Sir Henry St George, Clarenceaux King of Arms, to London.[35,77]

HERALDIC TAX

1798   An Act for granting to his Majesty a Duty on certificates issued in respect to armorial bearings or ensigns – from 1798.

Upon each piece of Vellum, Parchment or Paper upon which any certificate is issued to a person using or wearing armorial bearings
By any person keeping a coach and displaying arms   £2 2s 0d
By any person not keeping a coach but paying House or Window Tax and using arms   £1 1s 0d
By any person not keeping a coach or paying House or Window Tax but using arms   £0 10s 6d
Exemptions – the Royal Family or persons in service of or by appointment to it. Any City, Borough or Town Corporate.

1808   An Act for repealing the duties or Assessed Taxes and granting new duties in lieu and certain additional Duties etc. – 5 April 1808.

Duties payable by persons in respect of any armorial bearing or ensign used or worn by them
By any person keeping a coach and displaying arms   £2 8s 0d
By any person not keeping a coach but paying House or Window Tax and using arms   £1 4s 0d
By any person not keeping a coach or paying House or Window Tax but using arms   £0 12s 0d
Exemptions – the same as the 1798 Act

1861   Statute Law Revision Act – 1798 Armorial Bearing Act repealed

1869   Revenue Act
Duties to be levied for armorial bearings from 1 January 1870
If such armorial bearings be displayed on a carriage   £2 2s 0d
If such armorial bearings shall not be displayed but shall be otherwise worn or used   £1 1s 0d
Exemptions
1 The Royal Family and any person who by right of office uses the royal arms.
2 The sheriff of any county or mayor or other officer in any corporation or royal Burgh serving an annual office or any person by right of office who uses the arms of the corporation or Royal Burgh.
3 Any municipal or other corporation or any public company.

4 Any shopkeeper in respect of armorial bearings used solely as trademarks and in the course of trade.

5 Any officer or member of a club or society if the club or society has taken out an heraldic licence.

6 Any person residing in Ireland.[11 Vol 1,xxxi–xxxiii]

1899	£75347 Armorial tax collected by the Revenue.
1930/1	34379 Armorial Bearing licences taken out.

1944   Finance Act
Duties in respect of armorial bearings levied under the Revenue Act 1869 shall cease to be chargeable from 1 January 1945.

DECORATIONS and ORDERS

1348   Order of the Garter created by Edward III. Within a few years it became customary for Knights of the Garter to encircle their personal arms with the Garter.[20,263]

1469   Earliest extant Garter stall plate with arms encircled by a Garter is that of Charles the Bold, Duke of Burgundy.[18,Plate 75]

Other orders followed this practice from the date of their creation – *Detail of Garter Stall Plate of* with collars encircling the arms and other insignia suspended below. *Charles the Bold*

In the event of a person having more than one decoration or order the most senior was placed centrally, the next senior to the dexter, the next to the sinister and alternately outwards. Decorations and orders are not hereditary and can only be displayed during the lifetime of the holder or on any memorial commemorating him.

Establishment of Various British Orders and Decorations

Garter	1348	Royal Victorian Order	1896
Thistle	1687	Distinguished Service Cross	1901
Bath	1725	Order of Merit	1902
St Patrick	1783–1922	Imperial Service Order	1902
Royal Guelphic	1815–1837	Edward Medal	1907
St Michael & St George	1818	Military Cross	1914
Star of India	1851–1947	Companion of Honour	1917
Victoria Cross	1856	British Empire Order	1917
Albert Medal	1866	Distinguished Flying Cross	1918
Indian Empire	1878–1947	Air Force Cross	1918
Crown of India	1878–1947	Knight Bachelor's Badge	1929
Royal Red Cross	1883	George Cross	1940
Distinguished Service Order	1886		

Where a termination date is shown for an order no more awards were made after that date but previous holders could continue to wear the order until their death.

OFFICIAL and CORPORATE HERALDRY

Arms of Chester

Civic [3,13]

1329	Earliest known civic arms – City of Chester
18 Oct 1538	First grant of arms to a civic body – City of Gloucester
28 Aug 1561	First grant of a crest to a civic body – Borough of Ipswich
	First grant of supporters to a civic body – Borough of Ipswich
18 May 1889	First grant of arms to a County Council – West Sussex CC
27 Feb 1906	First grant of arms to an Urban District – Erith UDC
26 Mar 1906	First grant of a badge to a civic body – Borough of Launceston
23 Nov 1927	First grant of arms to a Parish Council – Bocking Parish Council
7 Jan 1938	First grant of arms to a Rural District – Wetherby RDC

Ecclesiastical [3,9]

1290	Earliest known arms of a See – See of Ely on the seal of Bishop William de Luda 1290–8
16 July1793	First grant of arms to a See – See of Quebec

Commercial [3,13]

10 Mar 1438/9	First grant of arms to a corporate body – The Drapers Company
15 Oct 1454	First grant of a crest to a corporate body – The Girdlers Company
7 Nov 1505	First grant of supporters to a corporate body – The Leathersellers Co.
30 Aug 1909	First grant of a badge to a corporate body – Port of London Authority

Academic

1 Jan 1449	Earliest grant of arms to an Academic establishment – Eton College and Kings College, Cambridge [3,9]
1905	First grant of arms to a University – Leeds [10,xii]

FLAGS

Late 11th C   Some of the earliest use of flags in this country are recorded on the Bayeux Tapestry.[5,249]

Pennons – small and pointed at the fly
Gonfanons – multi–tailed
The personal ensigns of a knight who bore them on his lance charged with his badge or armorial device
Mid 12th C   Both in use by this time [40,2]
1277   Pennon of Sir John D'Abernon displayed on brass at Stoke Dabernon.[5,250]
Mid 15th C   Gonfanons in use until this time but gradually replaced by the banner.[40,2]

Banners – square or oblong and charged with the arms of their owners – knights banneret, barons, princes and sovereigns.
1162   Banner used on seal of Philippe of Alsace.[40,8]
c1245   Some banners drawn in *Chronica Majora* by Matthew Paris.[30,66/7 & Pl I]

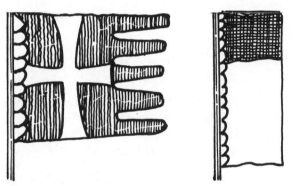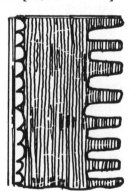

1300   Banners described in the siege of Caerlaverock poem

Standards – narrow, tapering and of considerable length – from four yards for a knight to eight to nine yards for the sovereign.[8,62]

Temp Edward   In use in this reign and in especial favour in Tudor times.[5,252]
III 1327–77

CHARGES

Earliest occurence of terms [2][31,103–113]

12th C	Argent	Azure	Cross	Or

13th C

Annulet	Chief	Fleur de	Indented	Molet	Rose
Bar	Cinquefoil	lys	Label	Orle	Roundel
Barry	Cotise	Flory	Leopard	Paly	Semy
Bend	Crescent	Formy	Lion	Party	Sable
Bezant	Crosslet	Fret	Lioncel	Passant	Saltire
Bezanty	Eagle	Fretty	Lozenge	Paty	Torteaux
Billet	Engrailed	Garb	Lozengy	Pile	Trefoil
Bordure	Ermine	Gemels	Lucy	Powdered	Tressure
Canton	Estoile	Gobony	Martlet	Quarterly	Vair
Chequy	Fer de	Gules	Mascle	Queue	Vert
Chessrook	Moline	Gyron	Masculy	Fourchy	Voided
Chevron	Fess	Gyronny	Maunch	Rampant	

14th C

Dexter	Fitchy	Fusil	Jessant de Lys	Pale	Sinister

15th C

Erased	Fimbriated	Flory–Counter–Flory	Nebuly	Pheon	Proper

16th C

Anchor	Bendlet	Couped	Langued	Plate	Sejant
Armed	Caboshed	Embowed	Ordinary	Quatrefoil	Statant
Attired	Compony	Enfiled	Passant–Gardant	Rampant–Gardant &	Trippant
Barbed	Counter–	Ermines	Patonce	Gardant &	Unguled
Barrulet	changed	Invected		Regardant	Volant

17th C

Gamb	Gorged

HERALDIC OFFICES

Purveyors of Arms to unsuspecting members of the public – or armsmongers, according to JP Brooke–Little, Richmond Herald.

1828 — Earliest mention found – Joshua Penny, Heralds College, Bennetts Hill, Doctors Commons, London – Robson's *London Directory* 8th Ed.

SAINTLY HERALDRY

c1245–61 — Arms of the Trinity (Matthew Paris – *Chronica Majora*) [30,61]
c1295 — Arms of St George (*Hours of the Virgin Mary* – Bodleian Library). [33,29]
c1400 — Arms for all the major saints established by this time.

APPENDIX

1	Bedingfield H & Gwynn–Jones P	Heraldry (1993)
2	Brault GJ	Early Blazon (1972)
3	Briggs G	Civic and Corporate Heraldry (1960)
4	Brooke–Little JP	An Heraldic Alphabet (1985)
5		Boutell's Heraldry (1973)
6	Cockayne GE	The Complete Baronetage (1983)
7	Fox Davies AC	The Art of Heraldry (1904)
8		Heraldic Badges (1907)
9		Complete Guide to Heraldry (1983)
10		The Book of Public Arms (1915)
11		Armorial Families (1929)
12	Franklin CAH	The Bearing of Coat Amour by Ladies (1923)
13	Franklin J	Shield and Crest (1960)
14	Friar S	A New Dictionary of Heraldry (1987)
15	Godfrey WH	The College of Arms (1963)
16	Haydn J	Dictionary of Dates (1857)
17	Heim B	Heraldry of the Catholic Church (1978)
18	Hope WHStJ	The Stall Plates of the Knights of the Order of the Garter (1901)
19		A Grammar of English Heraldry (1913)
20		Heraldry for Craftsmen and Designers (1913)
21	Huxford JF	Honour and Arms (1984)
22	Legh J	The Accidence of Armory (1591)
23	Murray H	'Shield Shape' Aspects of Heraldry 5, (1991)
24	Neubecker O	Heraldry – Sources, Symbols and Meaning (1976)
25	Parker J	A Glossary of Terms used in Heraldry (1894)
26	Pixley FW	A History of the Baronetage (1873)
27	Planché JP	The Pursuivant of Arms (1873)
28	Storry JG	Church and Heraldry (1982)
29	Summers PG	How to Read a Coat of Arms (1967)
30	Tremlett TD & London HS	Aspilogia II (1967)
31	Wagner AR	Historic Heraldry in Britain (1939)
32		Heralds and Heraldry in the Middle Ages (1939)
33		Heraldry in England (1946)
34		Aspilogia I (1950)
35		The Records and Collections of the College of Arms (1952)
36		Heraldry and Ancestors (1978)
37	Wise T	Medieval Heraldry (1980)
38	Woodcock T & Robinson JM.	The Oxford Guide to Heraldry (1988)
39	X (Fox Davies AC)	The Right to Bear Arms (1900)
40	Campbell C	Medieval Flags (Heraldry Society of Scotland)
41	Alexander J (ed)	Age of Chivalry (1987)
42	Kemp B	English Church Monuments (1980)